sand
between my
toes

Summer
Activity Book

by Erin Alladin

pajamapress

Let's write!

You're waking up for the best day of summer.
Make a list of the things you'll do.

Let's solve the puzzle! 💡

How many more beach balls are there than hot air balloons? Color the correct number.

2 1 4 3

Scavenger Hunt

Can you spot these things the next time you are out in the sun?

☐ Sun glasses

☐ A t-shirt with an animal picture

☐ Someone eating ice cream

☐ A bird

☐ A butterfly

☐ Sandals

Word search

**warm   sun   sand
summer   beach**

H	B	D	S	E	K
L	E	I	U	J	S
W	A	R	M	C	A
B	C	A	M	O	N
G	H	M	E	N	D
S	U	N	R	P	F

Let's color!

Color the **rabbit** and practice writing its name.

r a b b i t

Let's solve the puzzle!

Help **Queenie Quail** find her family.

Let's color!

Color the **hedgehog** and practice writing its name.

hedgehog

Let's draw!

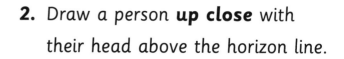

Make your drawings feel like real places!

1. Draw a **horizon line**.

That's the bottom of the sky.

2. Draw a person **up close** with their head above the horizon line.

3. Draw a person **far away**. Place their feet higher and their head lower down.

4. Treat trees, buildings, and objects the same way.

Now you draw!

Complete the silly story!

Choose each word from the box that matches the line.

Once upon a _, the

kingdom of _____ Ocean held

a sand _ _ _ _ _ _ _ _ _ _ _ _ _ _ _ _ - building contest.

Everyone ~~~~~~~~~~~~~~~~~~~ to the beach.

Some entries were _____. Some

were _____. Everyone thought

the _____ one would win until

a wave .... came

and ~~~~~~~~~~~~~~ along the sand. It swept

all the entries up into a _____

sand _ _ _ _ _ _ _ _ _ _ _ _ _ _ and won first place!

Adjectives

Huge
Pink
Funny
Spiky
Tiny
Useful
Wet

Adverbs

Sneakily
Grumpily
Eagerly
Slowly
Loudly
Hungrily
Messily

Nouns

Book
Cat
Squid
Soup Bowl
Spider
Planet
Tractor

Verbs

Danced
Raced
Fled
Jumped
Snuck
Jiggled

Let's match!

Match each object to its shadow.

Let's draw!

Decorate this girl's dress.

Let's solve the puzzle! 💡

Circle **5** differences in the pictures.

Sand Between My Toes

12345

Let's solve the puzzle!

Join the dots.

Let's color!

Color the snake and practice writing its name.

Let's draw!

Add your own **sandcastle** to the drawing.

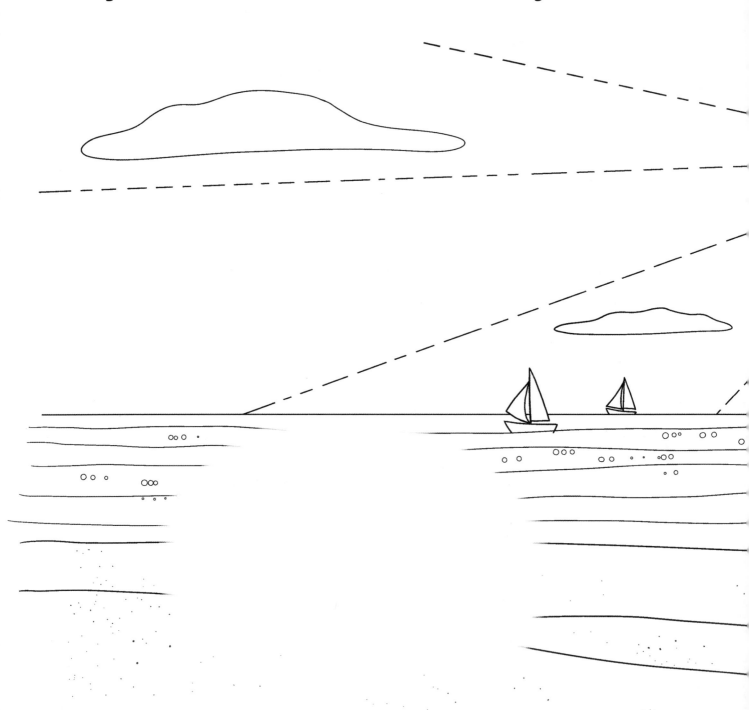

Sand Between My Toes

Let's solve the puzzle!

What comes next in the pattern?

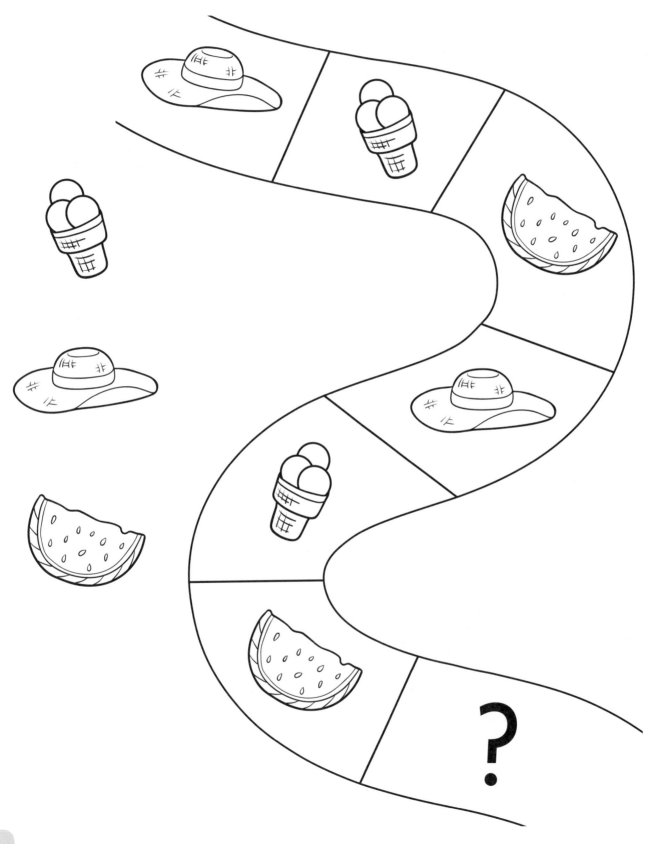

How Do You Roll?

Bicycle

Skateboard

Wheelchair

Scooter

Rollerblades

FOOD from the SUN

Plants are AMAZING.

They make their own food!

Using energy from the sun, they take apart air and water...

Everything we eat
depends on sugar from plants.

...and put the pieces
back together
to make **SUGAR.**

This plant superpower is called
PHOTOSYNTHESIS
(foh-toh-SIN-thuh-siss)

WHO LiVES iN THE GARDEN?

Dragonflies gobble lots of **mosquitoes.**

If **squirrels** can't find a shelter, they make **ball-shaped nests** from leaves.

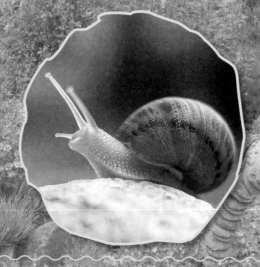

Snails come out at night and in the early morning, or on rainy days.

Toads like cool, damp hiding places, including upside-down **flower pots.**

Birds fertilize gardens with their rich droppings.

Ladybugs help gardeners by eating pest insects.

Butterflies often rest while hanging from the bottom of a leaf.

Garter snakes are gentle animals that like to rest in the sun.

Rabbits dig underground burrows.

Nature Art

The best craft materials **FOR** the earth...
come **FROM** the earth.

What can **YOU** find to inspire some *art*?

–Pack a–
Picnic!

Every culture has fun finger foods.
Which ones have you tried?

Pita bread has
a natural pocket inside
for holding ingredients.

Onigiri are balls of sticky rice
that are wrapped in seaweed
and stuffed with exciting flavors.

Sandwiches use two pieces
of sliced bread and...anything
you can fit between them!

Patties have tasty filling
surrounded by pastry so you
can hold it in your hand.

–Ways to Make a–
SANDCASTLE

1. Dribble very wet sand into shapes.

2. Use a bucket as a mold.

3. Sculpt the sand using your own hands.

What's YOUR favorite way to make a sand castle?

WHO CAN YOU FIND —AT AN— OCEAN BEACH?

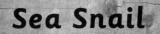
Sea Snail

Hermit Crab

Gull

Anemone

Kelp

Sand Dollar

Sea Star

WHO CAN YOU FIND

AT A

FRESH-

WATER

LAKE?

Heron

Racoon

Loon

Goose

Frog

Tadpole

Turtle

Minnow

What can you do with SIDEWALK CHALK?

Trace your friends and decorate inside the tracing

Play Tic-Tac-Toe

Try blending different colors

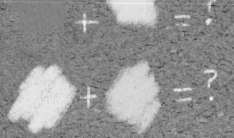

Play hopscotch

Draw a path for a friend to follow

START

30 20 10

you're DOING GREAT!

Make a target to play bean-bag toss

Leave encouraging messages for your neighbors

DiD YOU KNOW

Much of the art in this activity book comes from these wonderful books?

Sunny Days

Written by Deborah Kerbel
Illustrated by Miki Sato
ISBN: 9781772781977 (hardcover) | 9781772782530 (board book)
24 Pages

"Charming couplets about fun in the sun…. A multiracial array of children is shown in uncluttered, happy scenes filled with charming attention to detail."—**School Library Journal ★ Starred Review**

This is the Boat that Ben Built

Written by Jen Lynn Bailey
Illustrated by Maggie Zeng
ISBN: 9781772782424 (hardcover)
40 Pages

Young Ben's intrepid exploration of a northern river ecosystem (lovingly supervised by Mom).

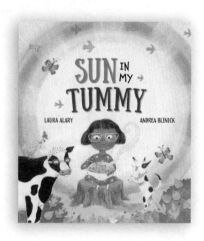

Sun in My Tummy

Written by Laura Alary
Illustrated by Andrea Blinick
ISBN: 9781772782417 (hardcover)
32 Pages

A mother describes to her young daughter how the sun's light becomes the energy in her body through the oats, blueberries, and milk in her home-cooked breakfast.

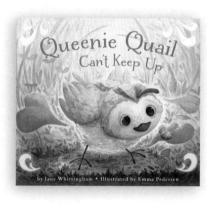

Queenie Quail Can't Keep Up

Written by Jane Whittingham
Illustrated by Emma Pedersen
ISBN: 9781772780673 (hardcover)
32 Pages

"Colors abound in green grass and clover, fluffy yellow chicks, and indigo-plumed parents as the quails learn a lesson from their littlest one about appreciating the beauty all around us."
—**Foreword Reviews**

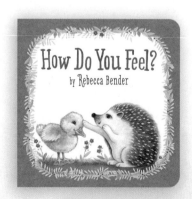

How Do You Feel?

Written and illustrated by Rebecca Bender
ISBN: 9781772780130 (hardcover)
32 Pages

"A charming, smart, and attractive book."
—**Kirkus Reviews**

"The ending of the book is a nice surprise—switching from a focus on physical feelings to emotional feelings."
—**CM Magazine**

Duck Days

Written by Sara Leach
Illustrated by Rebecca Bender
ISBN: 9781772781489 (hardcover)
104 Pages

"All readers will be able to relate to [Lauren's] experiences navigating friendships, child stresses at school, and big emotions."—**Youth Services Book Review**

Let's solve the puzzle!

Which route will take **Ben** to his dog?

Let's solve the puzzle!

Are these statements true or false?

1.   There are three children in the picture.   T / F

2.   All the children are wearing aprons.   T / F

3. There are two measuring scoops.   T / F

4. There are the same number of shovels and pails.   T / F

word search

hoop   ball   skip
throw   skate

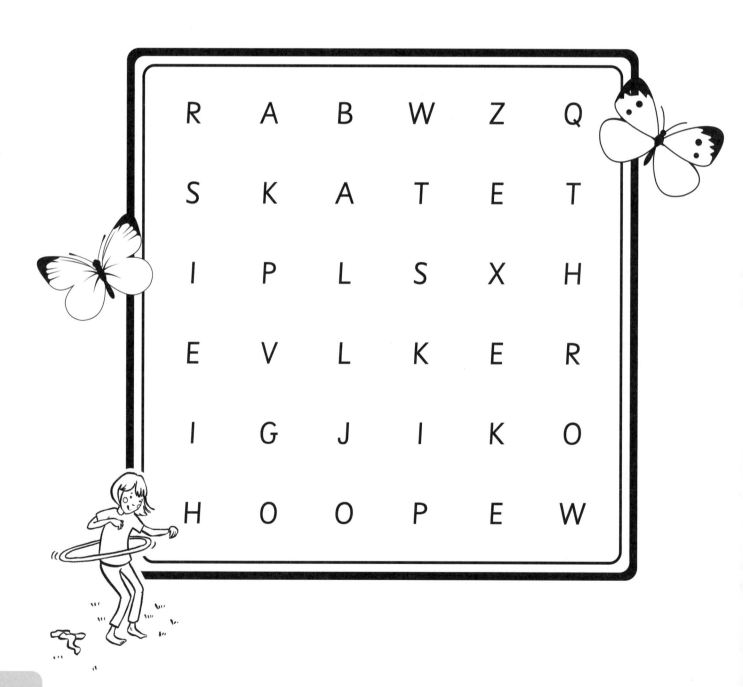

R	A	B	W	Z	Q
S	K	A	T	E	T
I	P	L	S	X	H
E	V	L	K	E	R
I	G	J	I	K	O
H	O	O	P	E	W

Let's solve the puzzle!

Choose the rhyming word to complete the poem.

off   away   around

I tried to catch a butterfly

One sunny summer's day.

It landed on my little nose

And then it flew _____!

Let's solve the puzzle!

How many **circles** can you find?

I found _____ circles.

Let's draw!

Learn to draw a **bicycle**.

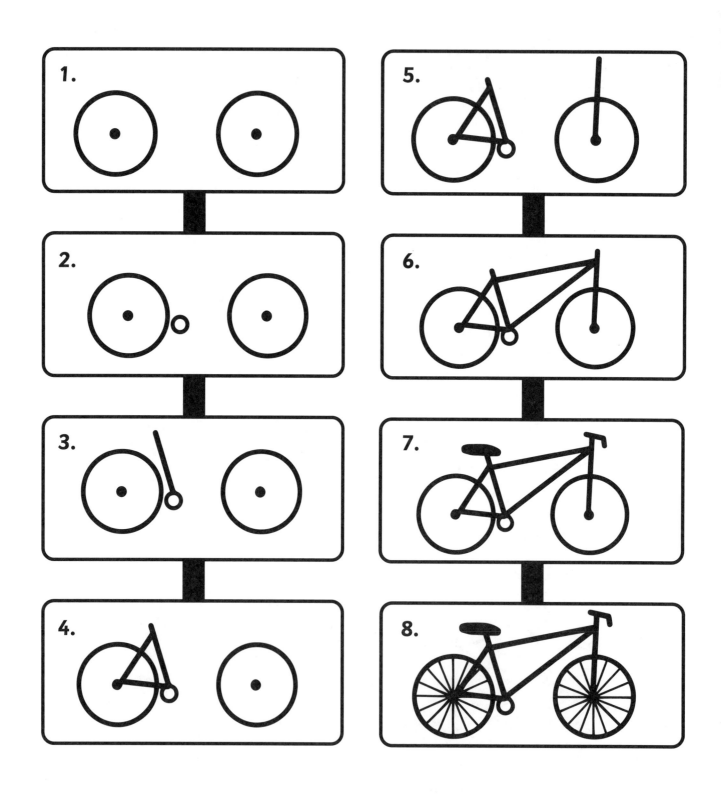

Now you draw!

Let's solve the puzzle! 💡

Solve the secret code.

⬭ = N	▢ = T	∘ = S
▭ = Y	☆ = E	◁ = O

D ◁ ⬭ ' ▢   F ◁ R G ☆ ▢

▭ ◁ U R

∘ U ⬭ ∘ C R ☆ ☆ ⬭ !

Let's draw!

How's the view?

Draw the **sun** rising outside the window.

Let's solve the puzzle! 💡

Help the **heron** find a fish to eat.

Let's solve the puzzle! 💡

How many **insects** can you find?

Let's match!

Match each **butterfly** to its shadow.

Let's color!

Color the **toad** and practice writing its name.

Let's solve the puzzle! 💡

Find the path up the mountain where every answer is **10**.

Complete the poem!

games   fun   friends

A blue sky,

A bright sun.

A perfect day

For summer _____!

Let's solve the puzzle!

Match each piece of **beach gear** to its name.

hat

sun glasses

sunscreen

bathing suit

sandals

Let's draw!

Draw yourself dressed up to go to the beach!

Let's draw!

Draw some **fish** in the **river**.

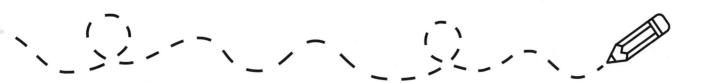

Let's solve the puzzle!

How many sticks do you need to...

...turn this **square** into two **rectangles**?

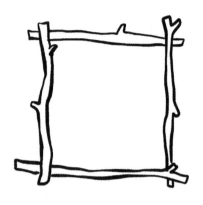

...turn this **triangle** into a **kite**?

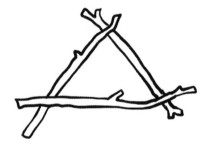

...turn this **rectangle** into four **triangles**?

Tip: You can try it out with real twigs or toothpicks!

Let's color!

Color the **snail** and practice writing its name.

snail

Let's draw!

What other **insects** live in tall grass? Add some to the picture.

Sand Between My Toes

Let's solve the puzzle!

Join the dots.